Everyday
Pocket

Beginners Spanish Phrase Book for Travelers of Spain and Other Spanish Speaking Countries

Vidal Alejandro

Copyright ©

Vidal Alejandro

© 2023 Spain

All rights reserved. No part of this book may be reproduced or modified in any form, including photocopying, recording, or by any information storage and retrieval system, without permission in writing from the publisher.

Table of Content

Copyright © 2
Vidal Alejandro 2
© 2023 Spain 2
Table of Content 3
Introduction 5
Spanish Phrases for Greetings and Basic Expressions 9
Spanish Phrases for Introducing Yourself 11
Polite Expressions 14
Spanish Phrases for Apologizing 16
Spanish Phrases for Basic Questions 18
Transportation: Airport and Flight 20
Taxi and Transportation Services 23
Bus and Train Transportation 25
Directions and Asking for Help 27
Hotel and Accommodation 31
Dealing with Issues and Complaints 34
Dining Out: Ordering Food and Drinks 37
Dietary Preferences and Allergies 40
Paying the Bill and Tipping 45
Basic Phrases for Shopping 49
Bargaining and Negotiating 54

Shapes and Colors 60

Expressing Preferences and Making Choices 63

Emergencies and Health 67

Emergency Services and Numbers 72

Describing Symptoms 75

Pharmacy and Medications 79

Leisure and Entertainment: Sightseeing and Tourist Attractions 83

Asking for Recommendations 87

Buying Tickets 90

Time and Weather 94

Days of the Week 100

Months of the Year 101

Seasons of the Year 102

Invitations and Accepting/Declining 103

Discussing Hobbies and Interests 107

Currency 110

Numbers 113

Animals 116

Flowers 119

Pronunciation Guide 121

Introduction

Whether you're planning a vacation, a business trip, or simply exploring the rich culture of Spanish-speaking countries, this handy phrase book is designed to be your trusted companion.

Packed with essential phrases, vocabulary, and useful expressions, it will help you navigate through various situations and communicate effectively with locals.

Why Spanish? Spanish is one of the most widely spoken languages in the world, with over 460 million native speakers spread across numerous countries, including Spain, Mexico, Argentina, Colombia, and many more.

By learning Spanish phrases, you open up a world of opportunities to connect with people, delve into local customs, and make your travel experiences more meaningful.

Some of its Key Features Include:

Compact and Portable: This phrase book is specifically designed to fit comfortably in your pocket, making it convenient to carry with you wherever you go.

Its compact size ensures easy access to essential phrases without the need for internet connectivity or relying solely on translation apps.

Everyday Situations: From basic greetings and introductions to navigating transportation, finding accommodation, ordering food, shopping, and handling emergencies, this phrase book covers a wide range of everyday situations that you're likely to encounter during your travels.

Each section is carefully organized to provide practical phrases and expressions to help you communicate effectively in different contexts.

Pronunciation Guide: Spanish pronunciation can be challenging for beginners. To help you sound more natural and confident, this phrase book includes a pronunciation guide for keywords and phrases.

With a clear understanding of pronunciation, you'll be able to communicate more effectively and be better understood by native speakers.

Remember, language is the key to unlocking cultural experiences and building connections with people from different backgrounds.

By making an effort to learn a few basic phrases in Spanish, you'll not only gain practical communication skills but also show respect and appreciation for the local culture.

Whether you're strolling through the vibrant streets of Barcelona, exploring the ancient ruins of Machu Picchu, or savoring the culinary delights of Mexico City, the Everyday Spanish Travel Pocket Size Phrase Book will be your reliable companion, helping you bridge the language barrier and make the most of your journey.

¡Buen viaje! (Have a great trip!)

Spanish Phrases for Greetings and Basic Expressions

Greetings - Saludos

Hello - Hola - (oh-lah)

Hi - Hola - (oh-lah)

Good morning - Buenos días - (bway-nos dee-as)

Good afternoon - Buenas tardes - (bway-nas tar-des)

Good evening - Buenas noches - (bway-nas no-ches)

How are you? - ¿Cómo estás? - (koh-moh es-tas)

How's it going? - ¿Cómo te va? - (koh-moh teh vah)

What's up? - ¿Qué tal? - (keh tahl)

Nice to meet you - Mucho gusto - (moo-cho goos-toh)

Goodbye - Adiós - (ah-dee-os)

See you later - Hasta luego - (ahs-tah loo-eh-go)

See you soon - Hasta pronto - (ahs-tah prohn-toh)

Have a nice day - Que tengas un buen día - (keh ten-gas oon bwehn dee-ah)

Take care - Cuídate - (kwee-dah-teh)

Welcome - Bienvenido/a - (byen-veh-nee-doh/dah)

Note: Spanish intonations are provided in parentheses as a guide to the general pronunciation, but it is recommended to listen to audio recordings or consult pronunciation resources for a more accurate understanding of the intonations.

Spanish Phrases for Introducing Yourself

Introducing Yourself - Presentación

My name is... - Me llamo... - (meh yah-moh)

I am... - Soy... - (soy)

Nice to meet you - Mucho gusto - (moo-cho goos-toh)

Pleased to meet you - Encantado/a - (en-kan-tah-doh/dah)

What's your name? - ¿Cómo te llamas? - (koh-moh teh yah-mahs)

Where are you from? - ¿De dónde eres? - (deh don-deh eh-res)

I'm from... - Soy de... - (soy deh)

How old are you? - ¿Cuántos años tienes? - (kwan-tos an-yos tee-ehnes)

I am ____ years old. - Tengo ____ años. - (ten-go ____ an-yos)

What do you do for a living? - ¿A qué te dedicas? - (ah keh teh deh-dee-kas)

I am a... - Soy... - (soy)

Where do you live? - ¿Dónde vives? - (don-deh vee-ves)

I live in... - Vivo en... - (vee-vo en)

Do you speak English? - ¿Hablas inglés? - (ah-blas een-gles)

Yes, I speak a little Spanish. - Sí, hablo un poco de español. - (see, ah-blo oon poh-ko deh es-pa-nyol)

What do you do for a living? - ¿A qué te dedicas? - (ah keh teh deh-dee-kas)

What are your hobbies? - ¿Cuáles son tus hobbies? - (kwa-les son toos oh-bees)

I enjoy... - Disfruto de... - (dis-froo-toh deh)

What is your favorite food? - ¿Cuál es tu comida favorita? - (kwal es too koh-mee-dah fa-voh-ree-tah)

My favorite food is... - Mi comida favorita es... - (mee koh-mee-dah fa-voh-ree-tah es)

Do you have any questions? - ¿Tienes alguna pregunta? - (tee-eh-nes ahl-goo-na pre-gun-tah)

Polite Expressions

Polite Expressions - Expresiones de Cortesía

Please - Por favor - (por fa-vor)

Thank you - Gracias - (gra-see-as)

You're welcome - De nada - (deh nah-dah)

Excuse me - Perdón / Disculpe - (per-don / dees-kool-peh)

I'm sorry - Lo siento - (loh see-en-toh)

May I...? - ¿Puedo...? - (pweh-do)

Could you please...? - ¿Podría por favor...? - (poh-dree-ah por fa-vor)

I would like... - Me gustaría... - (meh goo-sta-ree-a)

Sorry to bother you - Disculpa molestar - (dis-kool-pah mo-les-tar)

It was nice talking to you - Fue un placer hablar contigo - (foo-eh oon pla-ser ah-blar kon-tee-go)

Have a nice day - Que tengas un buen día - (keh ten-gas oon bwehn dee-ah)

Good luck - Buena suerte - (bweh-nah swer-teh)

Congratulations - Felicidades - (feh-lee-see-dah-des)

Excuse me for the inconvenience - Disculpe las molestias - (dees-kool-peh las mo-les-tee-as)

I appreciate your help - Aprecio tu ayuda - (ah-pre-see-o too a-yoo-dah)

Congratulations - Felicidades - (feh-lee-see-dah-des)

Spanish Phrases for Apologizing

Apologizing - Disculparse

I'm sorry - Lo siento - (loh see-en-toh)

I apologize - Me disculpo - (meh dees-kool-po)

Please forgive me - Por favor, perdóname - (por fa-vor, per-doh-nah-meh)

I didn't mean to - No fue mi intención - (no foo-eh mee een-ten-see-on)

I'm really sorry - Lo siento mucho - (loh see-en-toh moo-cho)

I regret my actions - Lamento mis acciones - (la-men-toh mees ak-see-oh-nes)

It's my fault - Es mi culpa - (es mee kool-pah)

I take full responsibility - Asumo toda la responsabilidad - (ah-soo-mo to-da lah re-spon-sah-bee-lee-dad)

Please accept my apologies - Por favor, acepta mis disculpas - (por fa-vor, ah-sep-tah mees dees-kool-pas)

I promise it won't happen again - Prometo que no volverá a suceder - (pro-meh-toh keh no vol-veh-rah ah soo-seh-der)

I deeply regret my mistake - Lamento profundamente mi error - (la-men-toh pro-fun-da-men-teh mee eh-ror)

I apologize for any inconvenience - Me disculpo por cualquier inconveniente - (meh dees-kool-po por kwal-kee-er een-kon-veh-nyen-te)

I'm truly sorry for the trouble caused - Lamento sinceramente los problemas causados - (la-men-toh seen-seh-ra-men-teh los pro-ble-mas kaw-sa-dos)

I'm sorry for the misunderstanding - Lamento el malentendido - (la-men-toh el ma-len-ten-dee-do)

I apologize for my behavior - Me disculpo por mi comportamiento - (meh dees-kool-po por mee kom-por-ta-myen-to)

Spanish Phrases for Basic Questions

What? - ¿Qué? - (keh)

Who? - ¿Quién? - (kyen)

Where? - ¿Dónde? - (don-deh)

When? - ¿Cuándo? - (kwan-doh)

Why? - ¿Por qué? - (por keh)

How? - ¿Cómo? - (koh-moh)

Which? - ¿Cuál? - (kwal)

Whose? - ¿De quién? - (de kyen)

How much? - ¿Cuánto/a? - (kwan-toh/a)

How many? - ¿Cuántos/as? - (kwan-tos/as)

Can I...? - ¿Puedo...? - (pweh-do)

Do you...? - ¿Tú...? - (too)

Is it...? - ¿Es...? - (es)

Are you...? - ¿Eres...? - (eh-res)

Did you...? - ¿Hiciste...? - (ee-cees-teh)

Where is...? - ¿Dónde está...? - (don-deh es-tah)

What time is it? - ¿Qué hora es? - (keh oh-rah es)

How far is...? - ¿Qué tan lejos está...? - (keh tan leh-hos es-tah)

Can you help me? - ¿Puedes ayudarme? - (pweh-des ah-yoo-dar-meh)

Are you sure? - ¿Estás seguro/a? - (es-tas seh-goo-ro/a)

Transportation: Airport and Flight

Airport and Flight - Aeropuerto y Vuelo

Airport - Aeropuerto - (ah-eh-ro-pwer-toh)

Flight - Vuelo - (bweh-loh)

Terminal - Terminal - (ter-mee-nal)

Gate - Puerta de embarque - (pwer-tah de em-bar-keh)

Boarding pass - Tarjeta de embarque - (tar-he-ta de em-bar-keh)

Security check - Control de seguridad - (kon-trol de seh-goo-ree-dad)

Customs - Aduana - (ah-doo-ah-nah)

Baggage claim - Recogida de equipaje - (reh-koh-hee-dah deh eh-kee-pah-he)

Departures - Salidas - (sah-lee-das)

Arrivals - Llegadas - (lye-gah-das)

Check-in counter - Mostrador de facturación - (mos-trah-dor de fak-too-rah-see-on)

Boarding - Embarque - (em-bar-keh)

Delayed - Retrasado/a - (reh-trah-sah-do/dah)

Canceled - Cancelado/a - (kan-seh-lah-do/dah)

Baggage - Equipaje - (eh-kee-pah-he)

Carry-on bag - Equipaje de mano - (eh-kee-pah-he deh mah-no)

Passport - Pasaporte - (pah-sa-por-teh)

Security screening - Control de seguridad - (kon-trol de seh-goo-ree-dad)

Flight attendant - Auxiliar de vuelo - (aw-ksee-lee-ar deh bweh-loh)

Pilot - Piloto - (pee-lo-toh)

Airline - Aerolínea - (ah-eh-ro-lee-neh-ah)

Reservation - Reserva - (reh-ser-vah)

Departure time - Hora de salida - (oh-rah deh sa-lee-dah)

Arrival time - Hora de llegada - (oh-rah deh lyeh-gah-dah)

Baggage allowance - Franquicia de equipaje - (fran-kee-see-ah deh eh-kee-pah-he)

Taxi and Transportation Services

Taxi - Taxi - (tah-ksee)

Driver - Conductor - (kon-dook-tor)

Car - Coche / Auto - (koh-che / ow-toh)

Bus - Autobús - (ow-toh-boos)

Train - Tren - (tren)

Metro - Metro - (meh-troh)

Station - Estación - (es-ta-syon)

Stop - Parada - (pa-ra-da)

Ticket - Boleto / Billete - (bo-le-to / bee-yeh-te)

Schedule - Horario - (o-ra-ree-oh)

Route - Ruta - (roo-ta)

Destination - Destino - (des-tee-no)

Pickup - Recogida - (reh-koh-hee-da)

Drop-off - Dejar / Bajar - (de-khar / ba-har)

Fare - Tarifa - (ta-ree-fa)

Meter - Taxímetro - (tak-see-meh-tro)

Airport shuttle - Servicio de transporte al aeropuerto - (ser-vee-syo de trans-por-te al ah-eh-ro-pwer-toh)

Ride-sharing - Compartir viaje - (kom-par-teer vee-a-he)

Public transportation - Transporte público - (trans-por-teh poo-blee-ko)

Taxi stand - Parada de taxis - (pa-ra-da deh tah-ksees)

Bus and Train Transportation

Bus - Autobús - (ow-toh-boos)

Bus stop - Parada de autobús - (pa-ra-da deh ow-toh-boos)

Bus station - Estación de autobuses - (es-ta-syon deh ow-toh-boos)

Bus route - Ruta de autobús - (roo-ta deh ow-toh-boos)

Bus ticket - Boleto de autobús - (bo-le-to deh ow-toh-boos)

Bus schedule - Horario de autobuses - (o-ra-ree-oh deh ow-toh-boos)

Bus driver - Conductor de autobús - (kon-dook-tor deh ow-toh-boos)

Train - Tren - (tren)

Train station - Estación de tren - (es-ta-syon deh tren)

Train ticket - Boleto de tren - (bo-le-to deh tren)

Train schedule - Horario de trenes - (o-ra-ree-oh deh tren-es)

Train platform - Andén de tren - (an-den deh tren)

Train conductor - Conductor de tren - (kon-dook-tor deh tren)

Train route - Ruta de tren - (roo-ta deh tren)

Train station agent - Agente de estación de tren - (a-hen-te deh es-ta-syon deh tren)

Train fare - Tarifa de tren - (ta-ree-fa deh tren)

Train departure - Salida de tren - (sa-lee-dah deh tren)

Train arrival - Llegada de tren - (lye-gah-dah deh tren)

Train platform number - Número de andén de tren - (noo-meh-ro deh an-den deh tren)

Train connection - Conexión de tren - (ko-nek-see-on deh tren)

Directions and Asking for Help

Directions - Direcciones - (dee-rek-see-oh-nes)

Map - Mapa - (mah-pah)

Street - Calle - (ka-yeh)

Avenue - Avenida - (ah-veh-nee-dah)

Turn - Girar - (hee-rar)

Left - Izquierda - (ees-kee-er-da)

Right - Derecha - (de-re-cha)

Straight - Derecho - (de-re-cho)

Intersection - Intersección - (een-ter-sek-see-on)

Traffic light - Semáforo - (se-ma-fo-ro)

Crosswalk - Paso de peatones - (pa-so deh pe-a-to-nes)

Stop sign - Señal de alto - (se-nyal de al-to)

Help - Ayuda - (ah-yoo-dah)

Can you help me? - ¿Puede ayudarme? - (pwe-deh ah-yoo-dar-me)

I'm lost - Estoy perdido/a - (es-toy per-di-do/a)

Where is...? - ¿Dónde está...? - (don-deh es-ta)

Could you repeat that? - ¿Podría repetir eso? - (po-dree-a re-pe-teer e-so)

I don't understand - No entiendo - (no en-tee-en-do)

Thank you - Gracias - (gra-see-as)

You're welcome - De nada - (deh na-da)

Can you show me on the map? - ¿Puede mostrarme en el mapa? - (pwe-deh mos-trar-me en el ma-pa)

Could you give me directions? - ¿Podría darme indicaciones? - (po-dree-a dar-me een-dee-ka-see-ones)

How do I get to...? - ¿Cómo llego a...? - (ko-mo lyeh-go ah)

I'm looking for... - Estoy buscando... - (es-toy boos-kahn-do)

Can you help me find...? - ¿Puedes ayudarme a encontrar...? - (pwe-des ah-yoo-dar-me a en-kon-trar)

Excuse me, where is the nearest...? - Disculpa, ¿dónde está el/la más cercano/a...? - (dees-kool-pah, don-deh es-tah el/la mas ser-kah-no/a)

Could you speak more slowly, please? - ¿Podrías hablar más despacio, por favor? - (po-dree-as a-blar mas des-pa-see-o, por favor)

Excuse me, can you help me? - Disculpa, ¿puedes ayudarme? - (dees-kool-pah, pwe-des ah-yoo-dar-me)

I need assistance - Necesito ayuda - (ne-se-see-to ah-yoo-dah)

Is there a... nearby? - ¿Hay un/una... cerca? - (ay oon/oona ser-ka)

Can you give me directions to...? - ¿Puedes darme indicaciones hacia...? - (pwe-des dar-me een-dee-ka-see-ones ha-sya)

Can you recommend a good...? - ¿Puedes recomendar un buen...? - (pwe-des re-ko-men-dar oon bwen)

Do you know where I can find...? - ¿Sabes dónde puedo encontrar...? - (sa-bes don-de pwe-do en-kon-trar)

Hotel and Accommodation

Hotel - Hotel - (o-tel)

Reception - Recepción - (re-cep-see-on)

Room - Habitación - (a-bee-ta-syon)

Reservation - Reserva - (re-ser-ba)

Check-in - Registro / Entrada - (re-his-tro / en-tra-da)

Check-out - Salida - (sa-lee-da)

Key - Llave - (ya-ve)

Front desk - Recepción / Mostrador - (re-cep-see-on / mos-trah-dor)

Bellboy - Botones - (bo-to-nes)

Concierge - Conserje - (kon-ser-he)

Single room - Habitación individual - (a-bee-ta-syon een-dee-vee-dual)

Double room - Habitación doble - (a-bee-ta-syon do-ble)

Suite - Suite - (swee-te)

Bed - Cama - (ka-ma)

Pillow - Almohada - (al-mo-a-da)

Blanket - Manta - (man-ta)

Towel - Toalla - (to-a-ya)

Bathroom - Baño - (ba-nyo)

Shower - Ducha - (doo-cha)

Wi-Fi - Wi-Fi - (wee-fee)

Breakfast - Desayuno - (de-sa-yu-no)

Restaurant - Restaurante - (res-tau-ran-te)

Room service - Servicio a la habitación - (ser-vee-syo a la a-bee-ta-syon)

Laundry - Lavandería - (la-van-de-ree-a)

Elevator - Ascensor - (as-see-sor)

Gym - Gimnasio - (heem-nah-see-oh)

Pool - Piscina - (pees-see-nah)

Parking - Estacionamiento - (es-tah-see-oh-nah-mee-en-toh)

Reception hours - Horario de recepción - (o-rah-ree-oh deh re-cep-see-on)

Dealing with Issues and Complaints

Issue - Problema - (pro-ble-ma)

Complaint - Queja - (keh-ha)

Problem - Incidencia - (een-see-den-syah)

Error - Error - (eh-rror)

Mistake - Equivocación - (eh-kee-vo-ka-see-on)

I have a problem - Tengo un problema - (ten-go oon pro-ble-ma)

There's a mistake - Hay un error - (ay oon eh-rror)

I'm not satisfied - No estoy satisfecho/a - (no es-toy sa-tees-fe-cho/a)

It's not what I expected - No es lo que esperaba - (no es lo keh es-pe-ra-ba)

Can you help me with this? - ¿Puedes ayudarme con esto? - (pwe-des a-yoo-dar-me kon es-to)

I would like to speak to a manager - Me gustaría hablar con el gerente - (me goos-ta-ree-a a-blar kon el he-ren-te)

Can I get a refund? - ¿Puedo obtener un reembolso? - (pwe-do o-ob-teh-ner oon re-em-bohl-so)

I need to file a complaint - Necesito presentar una queja - (ne-se-see-to pre-sen-tar oo-na keh-ha)

This is unacceptable - Esto es inaceptable - (es-toh es ee-na-sep-ta-ble)

I demand an explanation - Exijo una explicación - (eh-kee-ho oo-na eks-plee-ka-see-on)

I want to cancel my reservation - Quiero cancelar mi reserva - (kee-eh-ro kan-se-lar mee re-ser-ba)

I would like a different room - Me gustaría otra habitación - (me goos-ta-ree-a o-trah a-bee-ta-see-on)

I'm sorry for the inconvenience - Lamento la molestia - (la-men-toh la mo-les-tee-ah)

Can you fix it? - ¿Puedes arreglarlo? - (pwe-des a-rreh-glar-lo)

What can you do to resolve this? - ¿Qué puedes hacer para resolver esto? - (keh pwe-des a-ser pa-ra re-sol-ver es-to)

Dining Out: Ordering Food and Drinks

Menu - Menú - (meh-noo)

Table - Mesa - (meh-sah)

Waiter/Waitress - Camarero/Camarera - (ka-ma-reh-ro/ka-ma-reh-ra)

Order - Pedido - (pe-dee-do)

Appetizer - Entrante - (en-tran-teh)

Main course - Plato principal - (pla-toh prin-si-pal)

Dessert - Postre - (pos-treh)

Drink - Bebida - (be-bee-dah)

Water - Agua - (ah-gwah)

Wine - Vino - (vee-no)

Beer - Cerveza - (ser-ve-thah)

Coffee - Café - (ka-feh)

Tea - Té - (teh)

Can I see the menu, please? - ¿Puedo ver el menú, por favor? - (pwe-doh ver el meh-noo, por fa-vor)

What would you recommend? - ¿Qué recomendarías? - (keh re-ko-men-da-ree-as)

I would like to order... - Me gustaría pedir... - (me goos-ta-ree-a pe-deer)

I'm vegetarian/vegan - Soy vegetariano/vegano - (soy veh-he-ta-ree-a-no/veh-ga-no)

Is this dish spicy? - ¿Este plato es picante? - (es-teh pla-toh es pee-kan-teh)

Dessert menu - Carta de postres - (kar-tah deh pos-tres)

Ice cream - Helado - (eh-lah-doh)

Soft drink - Refresco - (reh-fres-ko)

Mineral water - Agua mineral - (ah-gwah mee-neh-ral)

Juice - Jugo - (hoo-go)

Can I have a glass of water, please? - ¿Me trae un vaso de agua, por favor? - (meh tra-eh oon ba-so deh ah-gwah, por fa-vor)

I would like the steak medium rare - Me gustaría el bistec poco hecho - (me goos-ta-ree-a el bee-stek poh-ko eh-cho)

Is there a vegetarian option? - ¿Hay alguna opción vegetariana? - (ay a-goo-nah op-see-on veh-he-ta-ree-a-na)

May I have the check, please? - ¿Puede traerme la cuenta, por favor? - (pwe-deh tra-ehr-meh la kwen-tah, por fa-vor)

Can I have the bill, please? - ¿Me trae la cuenta, por favor? - (meh tra-eh la kwen-tah, por fa-vor)

Dietary Preferences and Allergies

I'm vegetarian - Soy vegetariano/a - (soy veh-he-ta-ree-a-no/a)

I'm vegan - Soy vegano/a - (soy veh-ga-no/a)

I don't eat meat - No como carne - (no ko-mo kar-ne)

I don't eat dairy products - No consumo productos lácteos - (no kon-soo-mo pro-duk-tos lahk-tee-os)

I don't eat gluten - No consumo gluten - (no kon-soo-mo gloo-ten)

I have a food allergy - Tengo una alergia alimentaria - (ten-go oo-na a-ler-he-a a-lee-men-ta-ree-a)

I'm allergic to peanuts - Soy alérgico/a a los cacahuetes - (soy a-le-rgi-ko/a a los ka-ka-weh-tes)

I'm lactose intolerant - Soy intolerante a la lactosa - (soy in-to-le-ran-te a la lak-to-sa)

Do you have any vegan options? - ¿Tienen opciones veganas? - (tye-nen op-see-oh-nes veh-ga-nas)

Is this dish gluten-free? - ¿Este plato es sin gluten? - (es-te pla-toh es seen gloo-ten)

Are there any nut-free dishes? - ¿Hay platos sin frutos secos? - (ay pla-tos seen froo-tos se-kos)

Does this contain dairy? - ¿Contiene lácteos? - (kon-tee-neh lahk-tee-os)

Can you accommodate my dietary restrictions? - ¿Pueden adaptarse a mis restricciones alimentarias? - (pwe-den a-dap-tar-se a mis res-trik-syo-nes a-lee-men-ta-ree-as)

I'm allergic to shellfish - Soy alérgico/a a los mariscos - (soy a-le-rgi-ko/a a los mah-ree-skos)

Can you suggest a vegetarian dish? - ¿Puede sugerir un plato vegetariano? - (pwe-deh su-ge-reer oon pla-toh veh-he-ta-ree-a-no)

Gluten-free - Sin gluten - (seen gloo-ten)

Dairy-free - Sin lácteos - (seen lahk-tee-os)

Nut-free - Sin frutos secos - (seen froo-tos se-kos)

Shellfish - Mariscos - (mah-ree-skos)

Soy allergy - Alergia a la soja - (a-le-rgi-a a la soh-ha)

Corn allergy - Alergia al maíz - (a-le-rgi-a al mah-ees)

Egg allergy - Alergia al huevo - (a-le-rgi-a al weh-boh)

Wheat allergy - Alergia al trigo - (a-le-rgi-a al tree-go)

Sesame allergy - Alergia al sésamo - (a-le-rgi-a al se-sa-mo)

Fish allergy - Alergia al pescado - (a-le-rgi-a al pes-kah-do)

What options do you have for people with allergies? - ¿Qué opciones tienen para personas con alergias? - (keh op-see-oh-nes tyeh-nen pa-ra per-so-nas kon a-le-rgi-as)

Can you prepare a special meal for me? - ¿Puede prepararme una comida especial? - (pwe-deh pre-pa-rar-me oo-na ko-mee-da es-pe-syal)

Is this dish cooked with [ingredient]? - ¿Este plato está cocinado con [ingrediente]? - (es-te pla-toh es-ta ko-see-na-do kon [in-gre-dyen-te])

I have a severe allergy, so cross-contamination is a concern. - Tengo una alergia grave, así que la contaminación cruzada es una preocupación. - (ten-go oo-na a-ler-he-a gra-ve, a-see keh la kon-ta-mee-na-see-on kroo-sa-da es oo-na pre-o-ku-pa-see-on)

I appreciate your attention to my dietary needs. - Aprecio su atención a mis necesidades dietéticas. - (a-pre-see-o soo a-ten-see-on a mis ne-se-ee-da-des die-te-ti-kas)

When dining out, it's important to communicate your dietary preferences and allergies to ensure your needs are met.

However, it's also a good idea to inquire about ingredients and preparation methods to be extra cautious.

Paying the Bill and Tipping

Bill - Cuenta - (kwen-ta)

Check - Factura - (fahk-too-rah)

Cash - Efectivo - (eh-fek-tee-voh)

Credit card - Tarjeta de crédito - (tar-he-ta deh kre-dee-toh)

Debit card - Tarjeta de débito - (tar-he-ta deh dey-bee-toh)

Can I have the bill, please? - ¿Puede traerme la cuenta, por favor? - (pwe-deh tra-ehr-meh la kwen-ta, por fa-vor)

How much is it? - ¿Cuánto es? - (kwahn-toh es)

I will pay with cash/credit card. - Voy a pagar en efectivo/con tarjeta de crédito. - (voy a pa-gar en eh-fek-tee-voh/kon tar-he-ta deh kre-dee-toh)

Is service charge included? - ¿Está incluido el cargo por servicio? - (es-tah in-kloo-ee-do el kar-go por ser-vee-thyo)

Can I split the bill? - ¿Puedo dividir la cuenta? - (pwe-doh dee-vee-deer la kwen-ta)

Tip - Propina - (pro-pee-nah)

Service was excellent, here's a tip. - El servicio fue excelente, aquí tiene una propina. - (el ser-vee-thyo fwe ehks-seh-len-teh, a-kee tyeh-neh oo-nah pro-pee-nah)

Keep the change. - Quédate con el cambio. - (keh-da-teh kon el kam-bio)

The total is [amount]. - El total es [cantidad]. - (el to-tal es [kan-tee-dad])

What is the customary tip in this country? - ¿Cuál es la propina habitual en este país? - (kwahl es la pro-pee-nah ha-bee-twal en este pa-ees)

Can I pay separately? - ¿Puedo pagar por separado? - (pwe-doh pa-gar por se-pa-ra-do)

I would like to leave a tip. - Me gustaría dejar propina. - (me goos-ta-ree-a deh-har pro-pee-nah)

Service charge - Cargo por servicio - (kar-go por ser-vee-thyo)

Tax - Impuesto - (im-pwes-to)

Do you accept credit cards? - ¿Aceptan tarjetas de crédito? - (a-sep-tan tar-he-tas deh kre-dee-toh)

Is gratuity included? - ¿Está incluida la propina? - (es-tah in-kloo-ee-da la pro-pee-nah)

Could you bring the bill, please? - ¿Podría traer la cuenta, por favor? - (po-dree-a tra-ehr la kwen-ta, por fa-vor)

I will pay for everyone. - Yo pagaré por todos. - (yo pa-ga-reh por to-dos)

Keep the receipt, please. - Guarde el recibo, por favor. - (gwar-deh el re-see-boh, por fa-vor)

What's the total amount? - ¿Cuál es el monto total? - (kwahl es el mon-toh to-tal)

When paying the bill, you can indicate your payment preference and express your satisfaction with the service by leaving a tip.

Tipping customs vary by country, so it's helpful to inquire about the local practices or observe the norms around you.

Basic Phrases for Shopping

How much does it cost? - ¿Cuánto cuesta? - (kwahn-toh kwehs-tah)

I'm just browsing. - Solo estoy mirando. - (so-lo es-toy mee-ran-do)

Do you have this in a different color/size? - ¿Tienes esto en otro color/talla? - (tye-nes es-to en o-tro koh-lor/ta-ya)

Can I try it on? - ¿Puedo probármelo? - (pwe-do pro-bahr-meh-loh)

Do you have any discounts? - ¿Tienes algún descuento? - (tye-nes al-gun des-kwen-toh)

Can you show me something similar? - ¿Puedes mostrarme algo similar? - (pwe-des mos-trar-meh al-go see-mi-lar)

Is there a sale going on? - ¿Hay alguna oferta? - (ay al-gu-na o-fehr-tah)

I'll take it. - Me lo llevo. - (meh loh yeh-vo)

Can I get a receipt, please? - ¿Puedo tener un recibo, por favor? - (pwe-do te-ner oon re-see-boh, por fa-vor)

Where is the fitting room? - ¿Dónde está el probador? - (don-deh es-tah el pro-ba-dor)

What is your return policy? - ¿Cuál es su política de devolución? - (kwahl es soo po-lee-see-a deh de-voh-loo-syon)

Do you accept credit cards? - ¿Aceptan tarjetas de crédito? - (a-sep-tan tar-he-tas deh kre-dee-toh)

Can I get a discount if I buy more than one? - ¿Puedo obtener un descuento si compro más de uno? - (pwe-do ob-te-ner oon des-kwen-toh see kom-pro mas deh oo-no)

Is there a warranty on this item? - ¿Tiene garantía este artículo? - (tye-neh gahr-an-tee-ah es-te ar-tee-koo-lo)

I'm looking for [item]. - Estoy buscando [artículo]. - (es-toy boos-kahn-do [ar-tee-koo-lo])

Do you have this in stock? - ¿Tienen esto en stock? - (tye-nen es-to en stok)

What is the material/fabric? - ¿Cuál es el material/tela? - (kwahl es el ma-te-ree-al/teh-la)

Can you give me a better price? - ¿Me puedes dar un mejor precio? - (meh pwe-des dar oon me-hor pre-see-oh)

I'm looking for a gift. - Estoy buscando un regalo. - (es-toy boos-kahn-do oon re-gah-lo)

Can I see that one, please? - ¿Puedo ver ese, por favor? - (pwe-do ver e-seh, por favor)

It's too expensive. - Es demasiado caro. - (es de-ma-sya-do ka-ro)

I'm interested in buying. - Estoy interesado(a) en comprar. - (es-toy in-te-res-ah-do(a) en kom-prar)

Can I get a discount for cash payment? - ¿Puedo obtener un descuento por pago en efectivo? - (pwe-do ob-te-ner oon des-kwen-to por pa-go en eh-fek-tee-vo)

What are your store hours? - ¿Cuáles son sus horarios de atención? - (kwah-les son soos o-ra-ryos deh a-ten-see-on)

This doesn't fit me well. - Esto no me queda bien. - (es-toh no me keh-da byen)

Are there any sales or promotions? - ¿Hay alguna venta o promoción? - (ay al-gu-na ben-tah o pro-mo-see-on)

Can you recommend something? - ¿Puedes recomendarme algo? - (pwe-des re-ko-men-dar-meh al-go)

I'd like to exchange this. - Me gustaría hacer un cambio. - (me goos-ta-ree-a ha-ser oon kam-bee-o)

Can I get a refund? - ¿Puedo obtener un reembolso? - (pwe-do ob-te-ner oon re-em-bol-so)

Where is the nearest restroom? - ¿Dónde está el baño más cercano? - (don-deh es-tah el bahn-yo mas sehr-ka-no)

These phrases will come in handy while shopping and interacting with store staff.

Remember to be polite and feel free to ask for assistance or clarification whenever needed.

Bargaining and Negotiating

How much does it cost? - ¿Cuánto cuesta? - (kwahn-toh kwehs-tah)

Can you give me a discount? - ¿Me puedes hacer un descuento? - (meh pwe-des ha-ser oon des-kwen-to)

Is the price negotiable? - ¿Es el precio negociable? - (es el pre-see-oh ne-go-see-ah-bleh)

I can't afford that. - No puedo pagarlo. - (no pweh-doh pa-gar-loh)

What's your best price? - ¿Cuál es tu mejor precio? - (kwahl es too me-hor pre-see-oh)

I've seen it for a lower price elsewhere. - Lo he visto a un precio más bajo en otro lugar. - (loh eh vees-toh a oon pre-see-oh mas ba-ho en o-troh loo-gar)

Can we meet halfway? - ¿Podemos llegar a un acuerdo intermedio? - (po-deh-mos yeh-gar a oon a-kwer-do een-ter-meh-dee-oh)

Are there any special promotions or discounts? - ¿Hay alguna promoción o descuento especial? - (ay al-gu-na pro-mo-see-on o des-kwen-to es-pe-see-al)

Can you include any extras for the same price? - ¿Puedes incluir algún extra por el mismo precio? - (pwe-des in-kloo-eer al-gun eks-trah por el mees-moh pre-see-oh)

I'm a frequent customer. Can you offer me a better deal? - Soy un cliente frecuente. ¿Me puedes hacer una mejor oferta? - (soy oon klyen-teh fre-kwen-teh. meh pwe-des ha-ser oo-na me-hor ofer-tah)

Let's negotiate the price. - Vamos a negociar el precio. - (va-mos a ne-go-see-ar el pre-see-oh)

I'm interested, but I need a lower price. - Estoy interesado(a), pero necesito un precio más bajo. - (es-toy in-te-res-ah-do(a), pe-ro ne-se-see-to oon pre-see-oh mas ba-ho)

Can you match the price of your competitor? - ¿Puedes igualar el precio de tu competidor? - (pwe-des ee-gwah-lar el pre-see-oh deh too kom-pe-tee-dor)

55 | Everyday Spanish Travel Pocket Size Phrase Book

Let's find a win-win solution. - Encontremos una solución en la que todos salgamos ganando. - (en-kon-treh-mos oo-na so-loo-see-on en la ke to-dos sal-gah-mos ga-nan-do)

Can we discuss the terms? - ¿Podemos discutir los términos? - (po-deh-mos dis-ku-teer los ter-mos)

Can you give me a better price? - ¿Me puedes dar un mejor precio? - (meh pwe-des dar oon me-hor pre-see-oh)

I'm interested, but it's still too expensive. - Estoy interesado(a), pero aún es demasiado caro. - (es-toy in-te-res-ah-do(a), pe-ro a-oon es de-ma-sya-do ka-ro)

What's the lowest price you can offer? - ¿Cuál es el precio más bajo que puedes ofrecer? - (kwahl es el pre-see-oh mas ba-ho ke pwe-des o-fe-re-ser)

Let's find a compromise. - Encontremos un compromiso. - (en-kon-treh-mos oon kom-pro-mee-so)

Can you throw in any freebies or extras? - ¿Puedes incluir algún regalo o extras? - (pwe-des in-kloo-eer al-gun re-gah-lo o ek-strahs)

I'm a loyal customer. Can you give me a special discount? - Soy un cliente fiel. ¿Me puedes dar un descuento especial? - (soy oon klyen-te fee-el. meh pwe-des dar oon des-kwen-to es-pe-see-al)

Let's discuss the terms and conditions. - Vamos a discutir los términos y condiciones. - (va-mos a dis-ku-teer los ter-mos ee kon-dy-see-on-es)

Can we work out a better deal? - ¿Podemos llegar a un mejor acuerdo? - (po-deh-mos yeh-gar a oon me-hor a-kwer-do)

I'm comparing prices with other stores. - Estoy comparando precios con otras tiendas. - (es-toy kom-pa-ran-do pre-see-os kon o-tras tyen-das)

Can you match the price of your competitor? - ¿Puedes igualar el precio de tu competidor? - (pwe-des ee-gwah-lar el pre-see-oh deh too kom-pe-tee-dor)

Let's see if we can find a better offer. - Veamos si podemos encontrar una mejor oferta. - (ve-ah-mos see po-de-mos en-kon-trar oon-ah me-hor ofer-tah)

I'm interested, but I have a limited budget. - Estoy interesado(a), pero tengo un presupuesto limitado. - (es-toy in-te-res-ah-do(a), pe-ro ten-go oon pre-su-pwes-toh lee-mee-ta-do)

Is there any room for negotiation? - ¿Hay margen para negociar? - (ay mar-hen pa-ra ne-go-see-ar)

Can we find a middle ground? - ¿Podemos encontrar un punto intermedio? - (po-deh-mos en-kon-trar oon pwen-to een-ter-meh-dee-oh)

Let's work together to reach a mutually beneficial agreement. - Trabajemos juntos para llegar a un acuerdo mutuamente beneficioso. - (tra-ba-he-mos hun-tos pa-ra yeh-gar a oon a-kwer-do moo-twan-men-te be-ne-fee-see-oh-so)

Bargaining and negotiating skills can come in handy when shopping in markets or dealing with certain vendors.

Remember to be respectful, patient, and open to finding a mutually beneficial agreement.

Shapes and Colors

Shapes: - Forma

Circle - Círculo - (see-rkoo-lo)

Square - Cuadrado - (kwa-dra-do)

Triangle - Triángulo - (tree-ahn-goo-lo)

Rectangle - Rectángulo - (rehk-tahn-goo-lo)

Oval - Óvalo - (o-bah-lo)

Diamond - Diamante - (dee-ah-man-teh)

Heart - Corazón - (ko-rah-son)

Star - Estrella - (es-treh-yah)

Pentagon - Pentágono - (pen-tah-goh-no)

Hexagon - Hexágono - (heks-ah-goh-no)

Sphere - Esfera - (es-feh-rah)

Cone - Cono - (koh-no)

Cylinder - Cilindro - (see-leen-dro)

Crescent - Creciente - (kre-see-en-teh)

Cross - Cruz - (kroos)

Arrow - Flecha - (fle-cha)

Colors: - Color

Red - Rojo - (ro-ho)

Blue - Azul - (ah-sool)

Yellow - Amarillo - (ah-mah-ree-yo)

Green - Verde - (vehr-deh)

Orange - Naranja - (nah-ran-ha)

Purple - Morado - (mo-rah-do)

Pink - Rosa - (ro-sah)

Black - Negro - (neh-groh)

White - Blanco - (blahn-koh)

Gray - Gris - (grees)

Brown - Marrón - (ma-rrohn)

Gold - Oro - (oh-roh)

Silver - Plata - (plah-tah)

Beige - Beige - (be-eh-ge)

Turquoise - Turquesa - (toor-ke-sah)

Indigo - Índigo - (een-dee-go)

Magenta - Magenta - (mah-hen-tah)

Teal - Verde Azulado - (ver-de ah-soo-lah-do)

Lavender - Lavanda - (lah-vahn-dah)

Coral - Coral - (koh-ral)

Expressing Preferences and Making Choices

I prefer... - Prefiero... - (pre-fye-roh...)

I like... - Me gusta... - (meh goo-stah...)

I would rather... - Preferiría... - (pre-fe-ree-ree-ah...)

I enjoy... - Disfruto... - (dis-froo-toh...)

I love... - Amo... - (ah-moh...)

I'm a fan of... - Soy fanático(a) de... - (soy fa-na-tee-co(a) de...)

I'm interested in... - Me interesa... - (meh een-te-re-sah...)

I'm not really into... - No me llama mucho la atención... - (no meh yah-mah moo-choh lah a-ten-see-on...)

I don't like... - No me gusta... - (no meh goo-stah...)

I can't stand... - No soporto... - (no so-por-toh...)

My favorite... is... - Mi favorito(a)... es... - (mee fa-vo-ree-to(a)... es...)

I would choose... - Escogería... - (es-co-ge-ree-ah...)

If I had to pick... - Si tuviera que elegir... - (see too-vye-rah ke e-le-heer...)

I'm leaning towards... - Me inclino hacia... - (meh een-klee-no ah-syah...)

It's a tough choice, but I think I'll go with... - Es una decisión difícil, pero creo que me quedo con... - (es oo-na de-see-see-on dee-fee-seel, pe-ro creo ke meh keh-do kon...)

I would rather not... - Preferiría no... - (pre-fe-ree-ree-ah no...)

I have a preference for... - Tengo preferencia por... - (ten-go pre-fe-ren-see-ah por...)

My preference is... - Mi preferencia es... - (mee pre-fe-ren-see-ah es...)

I'm inclined to... - Estoy inclinado(a) a... - (es-toy een-klee-na-do(a) a...)

I'm leaning towards... - Me inclino hacia... - (meh een-klee-no ah-syah...)

I'm more inclined to... - Estoy más inclinado(a) a... - (es-toy mas een-klee-na-do(a) a...)

If I had to choose... - Si tuviera que elegir... - (see too-vye-rah ke e-le-heer...)

It's a tough decision, but... - Es una decisión difícil, pero... - (es oo-na de-see-see-on dee-fee-seel, pe-ro...)

I'm not particularly fond of... - No me agrada especialmente... - (no meh ah-grah-dah es-pe-see-al-men-te...)

I'm open to... - Estoy abierto(a) a... - (es-toy ah-byer-toh a...)

I'm considering... - Estoy considerando... - (es-toy kon-si-de-ran-do...)

I'm undecided between... - Estoy indeciso(a) entre... - (es-toy een-de-see-so(a) en-treh...)

I can't decide... - No puedo decidir... - (no pwe-do dee-see-deer...)

It's a tough call... - Es una decisión difícil... - (es oo-na de-see-see-on dee-fee-seel...)

Let me think it over... - Déjame pensarlo... - (deh-ha-me pen-sar-lo...)

Emergencies and Health

Help! - ¡Ayuda! - (ah-yoo-dah!)

Call the police! - ¡Llama a la policía! - (yah-mah ah lah po-lee-see-ah!)

Call an ambulance! - ¡Llama a una ambulancia! - (yah-mah ah oo-nah ahm-boo-lahn-see-ah!)

I need a doctor. - Necesito un médico. - (neh-seh-see-toh oon meh-dee-koh.)

Is there a hospital nearby? - ¿Hay un hospital cerca? - (ah-ee oon os-pee-tal sehr-kah?)

I'm feeling sick. - Me siento mal. - (meh see-en-toh mahl.)

I have an emergency. - Tengo una emergencia. - (ten-go oo-nah eh-mehr-hen-see-ah.)

I've been injured. - He resultado herido(a). - (eh re-sool-tah-do eh-ree-doh(a).)

I'm having difficulty breathing. - Tengo dificultad para respirar. - (ten-go dee-fee-kool-tahd pah-rah reh-spee-rar.)

I think I broke my arm/leg. - Creo que me rompí el brazo/pierna. - (kreh-oh keh meh rohm-pee el brah-soh/pyer-nah.)

I feel dizzy. - Me siento mareado(a). - (meh see-en-toh mah-reh-ah-doh(a).)

I'm allergic to... - Soy alérgico(a) a... - (soy ah-lehr-hee-koh(a) a...)

I need medication. - Necesito medicación. - (neh-seh-see-toh meh-dee-kah-see-on.)

Where is the nearest pharmacy? - ¿Dónde está la farmacia más cercana? - (don-deh es-tah lah fahr-mah-see-ah mas sehr-kah-nah?)

Can you please help me? - ¿Puedes ayudarme, por favor? - (pweh-des ah-yoo-dar-meh, por fa-vor?)

I'm feeling very ill. - Me siento muy enfermo(a). - (meh see-en-toh moo-ee en-fer-moh(a).)

I've lost consciousness. - He perdido el conocimiento. - (eh per-dee-do el koh-no-see-mee-en-toh.)

I think I'm having a heart attack. - Creo que estoy teniendo un ataque al corazón. - (kreh-oh keh es-toy te-nyen-doh oon ah-tah-keh al ko-rah-son.)

My friend needs medical help. - Mi amigo(a) necesita ayuda médica. - (mee ah-mee-go(a) neh-see-see-tah ah-yoo-dah meh-dee-kah.)

Is there a doctor available? - ¿Hay un médico disponible? - (ahy oon meh-dee-koh ah-vee-la-bleh?)

Where is the nearest clinic? - ¿Dónde está la clínica más cercana? - (don-deh es-tah lah klee-nee-kah mas sehr-kah-nah?)

I have a severe headache. - Tengo un fuerte dolor de cabeza. - (ten-go oon foo-ehr-te doh-lor deh ka-beh-sah.)

My child is injured. - Mi hijo(a) está herido(a). - (mee ee-ho(a) es-tah eh-ree-doh(a).)

I need an ambulance urgently. - Necesito una ambulancia con urgencia. - (neh-seh-see-toh oo-nah ahm-boo-lahn-see-ah kohn oor-hen-see-ah.)

Is there a pharmacy open at this hour? - ¿Hay una farmacia abierta a esta hora? - (ahy oo-nah fahr-mah-see-ah ah-byer-tah ah es-tah o-rah?)

I'm diabetic. - Soy diabético(a). - (soy dee-ah-beh-tee-koh(a).)

I need stitches. - Necesito puntos de sutura. - (neh-seh-see-toh poon-tos deh soo-too-rah.)

I have a high temperature. - Tengo fiebre alta. - (ten-go fee-eh-breh al-tah.)

I think I have food poisoning. - Creo que tengo intoxicación alimentaria. - (kreh-oh keh ten-go een-tox-ee-kah-see-on a-lee-men-tah-ree-ah.)

Can you call an ambulance for me? - ¿Puedes llamar a una ambulancia para mí? - (pwe-dehs yah-mar ah oo-nah ahm-boo-lahn-see-ah pah-rah mee?)

In case of emergencies or health-related situations, it's important to know how to seek help and communicate your needs.

Use these phrases to convey your situation and get the necessary assistance.

Emergency Services and Numbers

Emergency Services and Numbers – Servicios de Emergencia y Números

Emergency - Emergencia

Police - Policía

Ambulance - Ambulancia

Fire - Fuego / Incendio

Medical - Médico

Help - Ayuda

Call - Llamar

Accident - Accidente

Fire department - Bomberos

Poison control - Control de envenenamiento

Natural disaster - Desastre natural

Emergency exit - Salida de emergencia

Emergency room - Sala de emergencias

CPR (Cardiopulmonary Resuscitation) - RCP (Reanimación cardiopulmonar)

Emergency contact - Contacto de emergencia

Emergency Numbers in Spain:

Emergency Services (Police, Ambulance, Fire): 112

Police: 091

Medical Emergencies: 061

Fire Department: 080

Emergency Numbers in Mexico:

Emergency Services (Police, Ambulance, Fire): 911

Police: 060

Medical Emergencies: 065

Fire Department: 068

Remember, emergency numbers may vary by country. It's important to familiarize yourself with the local emergency numbers wherever you are traveling to ensure a prompt response in case of an emergency.

Describing Symptoms

I have a headache. - Tengo dolor de cabeza.

My throat is sore. - Tengo dolor de garganta.

I have a fever. - Tengo fiebre.

I feel dizzy. - Me siento mareado(a).

I have a cough. - Tengo tos.

My nose is congested. - Tengo la nariz congestionada.

I have a runny nose. - Tengo la nariz que moquea.

I have a stomachache. - Tengo dolor de estómago.

I feel nauseous. - Me siento nauseoso(a).

I have diarrhea. - Tengo diarrea.

I have a rash. - Tengo una erupción en la piel.

My muscles ache. - Me duelen los músculos.

I feel tired all the time. - Me siento cansado(a) todo el tiempo.

I have difficulty sleeping. - Tengo dificultad para dormir.

I feel shortness of breath. - Siento falta de aire.

I have chest pain. - Tengo dolor en el pecho. - (ten-go doh-lor en el peh-cho)

I feel weak and tired. - Me siento débil y cansado(a). - (meh see-en-toh deh-beel ee kahn-sah-doh(a))

I have a swollen ankle. - Tengo el tobillo hinchado. - (ten-go el to-bee-yoh een-chah-doh)

I have a persistent cough. - Tengo tos persistente. - (ten-go tohs per-see-sten-te)

I have difficulty swallowing. - Tengo dificultad para tragar. - (ten-go dee-fee-kool-tahd pah-rah trah-gar)

I feel a sharp pain in my back. - Siento un dolor agudo en la espalda. - (see-en-toh oon doh-lor ah-goo-doh en lah es-pal-dah)

I have a blister on my foot. - Tengo una ampolla en el pie. - (ten-go oo-nah am-poy-ah en el pyeh)

I have a persistent sore throat. - Tengo dolor de garganta persistente. - (ten-go doh-lor deh gar-gan-tah per-see-sten-te)

I have difficulty concentrating. - Tengo dificultad para concentrarme. - (ten-go dee-fee-kool-tahd pah-rah kon-sen-trar-meh)

I feel lightheaded and dizzy. - Me siento mareado(a) y con vértigo. - (meh see-en-toh mah-reh-ah-doh(a) ee kon ver-tee-go)

I have a burning sensation when I urinate. - Siento una sensación de ardor al orinar. - (see-en-toh oo-nah sen-sah-see-on deh ar-dor al oh-ree-nar)

I have frequent urination. - Tengo frecuencia urinaria. - (ten-go fre-kwen-see-ah oo-ree-nah-ree-ah)

I have a stiff neck. - Tengo el cuello rígido. - (ten-go el kwe-yoh ree-hee-doh)

I have watery eyes. - Tengo los ojos llorosos. - (ten-go los oh-hos yo-roh-sos)

I have a persistent fever. - Tengo fiebre persistente. - (ten-go fee-eh-bre per-see-sten-te)

When describing your symptoms, it's important to be as specific as possible to help medical professionals understand your condition better.

Additionally, seeking professional medical advice is recommended for accurate diagnosis and treatment.

Pharmacy and Medications

Pharmacy - Farmacia

Prescription - Receta

Medication - Medicamento

Pill - Pastilla

Tablet - Tableta

Capsule - Cápsula

Syrup - Jarabe

Ointment - Pomada

Cream - Crema

Drops - Gotas

Inhaler - Inhalador

Antibiotics - Antibióticos

Pain reliever - Analgésico

Allergy medicine - Medicina para las alergias

Antacid - Antiácido

Antihistamine - Antihistamínico

Cough syrup - Jarabe para la tos

Fever reducer - Reductor de fiebre

Prescription refill - Reposición de la receta

Over-the-counter - Sin receta / Sin recetario

I need to fill a prescription. - Necesito surtir una receta. - (neh-seh-see-toh soor-teer oo-nah reh-see-tah)

Is this medication available over the counter? - ¿Está disponible este medicamento sin receta? - (ehs-tah dee-soh-nee-bleh eh-steh meh-dee-kah-men-toh seen reh-see-tah)

What are the possible side effects? - ¿Cuáles son los posibles efectos secundarios? - (kwa-lehs son los poh-see-blehs eh-feh-tos seh-koon-dah-ree-ohs)

How often should I take this medication? - ¿Con qué frecuencia debo tomar este medicamento? - (kon keh freh-kwen-syah deh-boh toh-mar eh-steh meh-dee-kah-men-toh)

Are there any drug interactions I should be aware of? - ¿Existen interacciones medicamentosas que deba tener en cuenta? - (ehk-see-sten een-teh-rak-see-oh-nes meh-dee-kah-men-toh-sahs keh deh-bah teh-ner en koon-tah)

Can I get a generic version of this medication? - ¿Puedo obtener una versión genérica de este medicamento? - (pweh-doh oh-beh-ner oo-nah behr-see-on heh-neh-ree-kah deh eh-steh meh-dee-kah-men-toh)

I am allergic to penicillin. - Soy alérgico(a) a la penicilina. - (soy ah-lehr-hee-koh(ah) ah lah peh-nee-see-lee-nah)

Please label the medication with the dosage instructions. - Por favor, etiquete el medicamento con las instrucciones de dosis. - (por fah-vor, eh-tee-keh-teh el meh-dee-kah-men-toh kon las een-strook-see-oh-nes deh doh-sees)

What is the expiration date of this medication? - ¿Cuál es la fecha de vencimiento de este medicamento? - (kwal es lah feh-chah deh ben-see-mee-en-toh deh eh-steh meh-dee-kah-men-toh)

Can I get a receipt for this purchase? - ¿Puedo obtener un recibo por esta compra? - (pweh-doh oh-beh-ner oon reh-see-boh por es-tah kohm-prah)

When visiting a pharmacy, it's important to have your prescription or a clear description of your symptoms to help the pharmacist provide you with the appropriate medication.

If you are unsure about the dosage or any instructions, don't hesitate to ask the pharmacist for clarification.

Leisure and Entertainment: Sightseeing and Tourist Attractions

Cinema - Cine - (see-neh)

Theater - Teatro - (teh-ah-troh)

Concert - Concierto - (kohn-see-ehr-toh)

Museum - Museo - (moo-seh-oh)

Art gallery - Galería de arte - (gah-leh-ree-ah deh ah-reh-teh)

Park - Parque - (pahr-keh)

Beach - Playa - (plah-yah)

Zoo - Zoológico - (zoh-oh-loh-hee-koh)

Amusement park - Parque de atracciones - (pahr-keh deh ah-trahk-see-oh-nes)

Sports stadium - Estadio deportivo - (eh-stah-dee-oh deh-por-tee-boh)

Shopping mall - Centro comercial - (sen-troh koh-mehr-see-ahl)

83 | Everyday Spanish Travel Pocket Size Phrase Book

Bowling alley - Bolera - (boh-leh-rah)

Arcade - Sala de juegos - (sah-lah deh hweh-gohs)

Nightclub - Discoteca - (dees-koh-teh-kah)

Pub - Bar - (bar)

Restaurant - Restaurante - (res-tow-ran-teh)

Café - Café - (ka-feh)

Live music - Música en vivo - (moo-see-kah en vee-boh)

Dance performance - Espectáculo de baile - (eh-spehk-tah-koo deh bahy-leh)

Outdoor activities - Actividades al aire libre - (ahk-tee-vee-dah-des ahl ahy-reh lee-breh)

Swimming pool - Piscina - (pee-see-nah)

Hiking - Senderismo - (sehn-deh-rees-moh)

Cycling - Ciclismo - (see-klees-moh)

Fishing - Pesca - (pehs-kah)

Picnic - Picnic - (peek-neek)

Sightseeing - Turismo - (too-ris-moh)

Photography - Fotografía - (foh-toh-grah-fee-ah)

Reading - Lectura - (lehk-too-rah)

Karaoke - Karaoke - (kah-rah-oh-keh)

Board games - Juegos de mesa - (hweh-gohs deh meh-sah)

Concert - Concierto - (kohn-see-ehr-toh)

Comedy show - Espectáculo de comedia - (eh-spehk-tah-koo deh koh-meh-dee-ah)

Dance class - Clase de baile - (klah-seh deh bahy-leh)

Yoga - Yoga - (yoh-gah)

Cooking class - Clase de cocina - (klah-seh deh koh-see-nah)

Wine tasting - Cata de vinos - (kah-tah deh vee-nohs)

Movie night - Noche de películas - (noh-cheh deh peh-lee-koo-lahs)

Art workshop - Taller de arte - (tah-yehr deh ah-reh-teh)

Theater play - Obra de teatro - (oh-brah deh teh-ah-troh)

Dance party - Fiesta de baile - (fee-ehs-tah deh bahy-leh)

These words and phrases can be useful when talking about leisure and entertainment options or when asking for recommendations during your travels.

Asking for Recommendations

Can you recommend...? - ¿Puede recomendar...? - (pweh-deh reh-koh-mehn-dahr)

Any good...? - ¿Algún buen...? - (ahl-goon bwehn)

What are some...? - ¿Cuáles son algunos...? - (kwah-lehs sohn ahl-goo-nohs)

Do you have any suggestions...? - ¿Tiene alguna sugerencia...? - (tyeh-neh ahl-goo-nah soo-heh-rehn-see-ah)

Where can I find...? - ¿Dónde puedo encontrar...? - (don-deh pweh-doh ehn-kohn-trahr)

Are there any...? - ¿Hay algún...? - (ai ahl-goon)

Which... would you recommend...? - ¿Cuál... recomendaría...? - (kwahl reh-koh-mehn-dah-ree-ah)

Is there a particular...? - ¿Hay algún... en particular? - (ai ahl-goon ehn pahr-tee-koo-lahr)

Can you suggest...? - ¿Puede sugerir...? - (pweh-deh soo-heh-reer)

What are some must-see...? - ¿Cuáles son algunos lugares imperdibles...? - (kwah-lehs sohn ahl-goo-nohs loo-gah-rehs eem-pehr-dee-blehs)

What's your favorite...? - ¿Cuál es tu... favorito/a? - (kwahl ehs too... fah-voh-ree-toh/ah)

I'm looking for... - Estoy buscando... - (ehs-toy boos-kahn-doh)

Any recommendations for...? - ¿Alguna recomendación para...? - (ahl-goo-nah reh-koh-mehn-dah-see-ohn pah-rah)

Where should I go to...? - ¿Dónde debo ir para...? - (don-deh deh-boh eer pah-rah)

Can you suggest a good place to...? - ¿Puedes sugerir un buen lugar para...? - (pweh-dehs soo-heh-reer oon bwehn loo-gahr pah-rah)

Is there a famous... around here? - ¿Hay algún... famoso por aquí? - (ai ahl-goon... fah-moh-soh por ah-kee)

Do you know any hidden gems...? - ¿Conoces algún tesoro escondido...? - (koh-noh-ces ahl-goon teh-soh-roh ehs-kohn-dee-doh)

Are there any local specialties...? - ¿Existen especialidades locales...? - (ehk-see-stehn es-peh-see-ah-lee-dah-dehs loh-kah-lehs)

What's the best time to...? - ¿Cuál es el mejor momento para...? - (kwahl ehs ehl meh-hor moh-men-toh pah-rah)

Are there any discounts or deals...? - ¿Hay algún descuento o oferta...? - (ai ahl-goon dehs-kooehn-toh oh oh-fehr-tah)

Buying Tickets

How much does a ticket cost? - ¿Cuánto cuesta un boleto? - (kwahn-toh kwehs-tah oon boh-leh-toh)

Are there any discounts available? - ¿Hay algún descuento disponible? - (ai ahl-goon dehs-kooehn-toh dee-soh-nee-blay)

Can I buy tickets online? - ¿Puedo comprar boletos en línea? - (pweh-doh kohm-prahr boh-leh-tohs ehn lee-nyah)

Where is the ticket office? - ¿Dónde está la taquilla? - (don-deh ehs-tah lah tah-kee-yah)

Is it possible to reserve tickets in advance? - ¿Es posible reservar boletos con antelación? - (ehs poh-see-bleh reh-sehr-bahr boh-leh-tohs kohn ahn-teh-lah-see-ohn)

Do I need to show ID to purchase a ticket? - ¿Necesito mostrar identificación para comprar un boleto? - (neh-seh-see-toh mohs-trahr een-tee-fee-kah-see-ohn pah-rah kohm-prahr oon boh-leh-toh)

Are there different ticket options available? - ¿Hay diferentes opciones de boletos disponibles? - (ai ahl-goon-ehs ohp-see-oh-ness deh boh-leh-tohs dee-soh-nee-blays)

Can I get a refund if I can't attend the event? - ¿Puedo obtener un reembolso si no puedo asistir al evento? - (pweh-doh ohb-teh-nehr oon reh-ehm-bohl-soh see noh pweh-doh ah-see-teer ahl eh-vehn-toh)

How can I pay for the tickets? - ¿Cómo puedo pagar los boletos? - (koh-moh pweh-doh pah-gahr lohs boh-leh-tohs)

Do children have discounted tickets? - ¿Los niños tienen boletos con descuento? - (lohs nyeh-nyohs tyeh-nehn boh-leh-tohs kohn dehs-kooehn-toh)

How can I get tickets for...? - ¿Cómo puedo obtener boletos para...? - (koh-moh pweh-doh ohb-teh-nehr boh-leh-tohs pah-rah)

Are there any student discounts? - ¿Hay descuentos para estudiantes? - (ai ayl dehs-kooehn-tohs pah-rah ehs-too-dee-yahn-tehs)

Can I buy tickets at the door? - ¿Puedo comprar boletos en la puerta? - (pweh-doh kohm-prahr boh-leh-tohs ehn lah pwer-tah)

Is there a limit to the number of tickets I can purchase? - ¿Hay un límite en el número de boletos que puedo comprar? - (ai ayn lee-mee-teh ehn ehl noo-meh-roh deh boh-leh-tohs keh pweh-doh kohm-prahr)

Do I need to print the tickets or can I show them on my phone? - ¿Necesito imprimir los boletos o puedo mostrarlos en mi teléfono? - (neh-seh-see-toh eem-pree-meer lohs boh-leh-tohs oh pweh-doh mohs-trahr-los ehn mee teh-leh-foh-noh)

Are there any VIP or premium ticket options? - ¿Hay opciones de boletos VIP o premium? - (ai ayl ohp-see-yoh-nehs deh boh-leh-tohs VIP oh preh-mee-oom)

Can I upgrade my ticket to a higher category? - ¿Puedo mejorar mi boleto a una categoría superior? - (pweh-doh meh-yoh-rahr mee boh-leh-toh ah oo-nah kah-teh-goh-ree-ah soo-pee-ohr)

Are there any group discounts available? - ¿Hay descuentos para grupos disponibles? - (ai ayl dehs-kooehn-tohs pah-rah groo-pohs dee-soh-nee-blays)

Can I change the date or time of my ticket? - ¿Puedo cambiar la fecha o la hora de mi boleto? - (pweh-doh kahm-bee-ar lah feh-cha oh lah oh-rah deh mee boh-leh-toh)

Is there a box office where I can buy tickets in person? - ¿Hay una taquilla donde pueda comprar boletos en persona? - (ai oo-nah tah-kee-yah dohn-deh pweh-dah kohm-prahr boh-leh-tohs ehn pehr-soh-nah)

Time and Weather

What time is it? - ¿Qué hora es? - (keh oh-rah ehs)

It's [time] o'clock. - Son las [hora] en punto. - (sohn las [oh-rah] ehn poon-toh)

What's the date today? - ¿Cuál es la fecha de hoy? - (kwahl ehs lah feh-cha deh oy)

What day is it today? - ¿Qué día es hoy? - (keh dee-ah ehs oy)

Is it morning, afternoon, or evening? - ¿Es de mañana, tarde o noche? - (ehs deh mah-nyah-nah, tar-deh oh noh-cheh)

What's the weather like today? - ¿Cómo está el clima hoy? - (koh-moh ehs-tah ehl klee-mah oy)

Is it hot/cold outside? - ¿Hace calor/frío afuera? - (ah-seh kah-lohr/free-oh ah-fwehr-ah)

It's sunny/cloudy/rainy. - Hace sol/está nublado/llueve. - (ah-seh sohl/ehs-tah noo-blah-doh-yoh/you-eh-veh)

What's the temperature? - ¿Cuál es la temperatura? - (kwahl ehs lah tehm-peh-rah-too-rah)

What time does [event/activity] start? - ¿A qué hora comienza [evento/actividad]? - (ah keh oh-rah koh-mee-en-sah [eh-ven-toh/ahk-tee-vee-dahd])

How long does it take to get there? - ¿Cuánto tiempo se tarda en llegar? - (kwahn-toh tee-ehm-poh seh tar-dah ehn yeh-gar)

It's early/late. - Es temprano/tarde. - (ehs tehm-prah-noh/tar-deh)

What's the forecast for tomorrow? - ¿Cuál es el pronóstico para mañana? - (kwahl ehs ehl proh-nos-tee-koh pah-rah mah-nyah-nah)

Is it going to rain/snow? - ¿Va a llover/nevar? - (bah ah yo-ver/neh-var)

The weather is pleasant. - El clima es agradable. - (ehl klee-mah ehs ah-grah-dah-bleh)

It's windy. - Hace viento. - (ah-seh vyen-toh)

What's the humidity level? - ¿Cuál es el nivel de humedad? - (kwahl ehs ehl nee-vel deh oo-meh-dad)

Is there a chance of thunderstorms? - ¿Hay posibilidad de tormentas? - (ai poh-see-bee-lee-dad deh tor-men-tahs)

The sun is shining. - El sol está brillando. - (ehl sohl ehs-tah bree-yahn-doh)

Time - Tiempo - (tee-ehm-poh)

Hour - Hora - (oh-rah)

Minute - Minuto - (mee-noo-toh)

Second - Segundo - (seh-goon-doh)

Day - Día - (dee-ah)

Week - Semana - (seh-mah-nah)

Month - Mes - (mehs)

Year - Año - (ahn-yoh)

Morning - Mañana - (mah-nyah-nah)

Afternoon - Tarde - (tar-deh)

Evening - Noche - (noh-cheh)

Midnight - Medianoche - (meh-dee-ah-noh-cheh)

Today - Hoy - (oy)

Yesterday - Ayer - (ah-yehr)

Tomorrow - Mañana - (mah-nyah-nah)

AM - de la mañana - (deh lah mah-nyah-nah)

PM - de la tarde/noche - (deh lah tar-deh/noh-cheh)

Clock - Reloj - (reh-loh)

Watch - Reloj de pulsera - (reh-loh deh pool-seh-rah)

Time zone - Zona horaria - (soh-nah oh-rah-ree-ah)

Schedule - Horario - (oh-rah-ree-oh)

Appointment - Cita - (see-tah)

Deadline - Fecha límite - (feh-cha lee-mee-teh)

Duration - Duración - (doo-rah-see-ohn)

Stopwatch - Cronómetro - (kroh-noh-meh-troh)

Calendar - Calendario - (cah-len-dah-ree-oh)

Season - Temporada - (tem-poh-rah-dah)

Clockwise - En sentido de las agujas del reloj - (ehn sehn-tee-doh deh las ah-goo-hahs del reh-loh)

Counterclockwise - En sentido contrario a las agujas del reloj - (ehn sehn-tee-doh kohn-trah-ree-oh ah las ah-goo-hahs del reh-loh)

Delay - Retraso - (reh-trah-soh)

Early - Temprano - (tehm-prah-noh)

Late - Tarde - (tar-deh)

Past - Pasado - (pah-sah-doh)

Present - Presente - (preh-zen-teh)

Future - Futuro - (foo-too-roh)

Timetable - Horario - (oh-rah-ree-oh)

Days of the Week

Monday - Lunes - (loo-nes)

Tuesday - Martes - (mar-tes)

Wednesday - Miércoles - (mee-ehr-coh-les)

Thursday - Jueves - (hweh-ves)

Friday - Viernes - (vee-ehr-nes)

Saturday - Sábado - (sah-bah-doh)

Sunday - Domingo - (doh-meen-goh)

These words will help you refer to specific days of the week in Spanish conversations.

Months of the Year

January - Enero - (eh-neh-roh)

February - Febrero - (feh-breh-roh)

March - Marzo - (mar-thoh)

April - Abril - (ah-breel)

May - Mayo - (mah-yoh)

June - Junio - (hoo-nee-oh)

July - Julio - (hoo-lee-oh)

August - Agosto - (ah-gohs-toh)

September - Septiembre - (sep-tyem-breh)

October - Octubre - (ohk-too-breh)

November - Noviembre - (noh-vee-yem-breh)

December - Diciembre - (dee-see-yem-breh)

These words will help you refer to specific months of the year in Spanish conversations.

Seasons of the Year

Spring - Primavera - (pree-mah-veh-rah)

Summer - Verano - (veh-rah-noh)

Autumn/Fall - Otoño - (oh-toh-nyoh)

Winter - Invierno - (een-vyehr-noh)

These words will help you refer to the different seasons of the year in Spanish conversations.

Invitations and Accepting/Declining

Invitation - Invitación - (een-vee-tah-see-ohn)

Party - Fiesta - (fee-es-tah)

Event - Evento - (eh-ven-toh)

Gathering - Reunión - (reh-oo-nyon)

Celebrate - Celebrar - (se-leh-brar)

Join us - Únete a nosotros - (oo-neh-teh ah noh-soh-tros)

Come to - Ven a - (ven ah)

Please join us - Por favor, únete a nosotros - (por fah-vor, oo-neh-teh ah noh-soh-tros)

You're invited - Estás invitado/a - (ehs-tahs een-vee-tah-doh/dah)

Can you come? - ¿Puedes venir? - (pweh-des veh-neer)

Accept - Aceptar - (ah-sep-tar)

Yes, I'll come - Sí, voy a venir - (see, voy ah veh-neer)

Sure, I'd love to - Claro, me encantaría - (kla-roh, meh ehn-kahn-tah-ree-ah)

Decline - Declinar - (deh-klee-nar)

Sorry, I can't make it - Lo siento, no puedo ir - (loh see-ehn-toh, noh pweh-doh eer)

Unfortunately, I have other plans - Desafortunadamente, tengo otros planes - (deh-sah-for-tu-nah-dah-men-teh, ten-go oh-tros plan-es)

Maybe next time - Quizás la próxima vez - (kee-sas lah proh-see-mah behs)

Thank you for the invitation - Gracias por la invitación - (grah-see-as por lah een-vee-tah-see-ohn)

It sounds great, but I'm busy - Suena genial, pero estoy ocupado/a - (sweh-nah heh-nee-al, peh-roh es-toy oh-koo-pah-doh/dah)

I'll let you know - Te aviso - (teh ah-vee-soh)

104 | Everyday Spanish Travel Pocket Size Phrase Book

Are you free on [date/time]? - ¿Estás libre el [fecha/hora]? - (ehs-tahs lee-breh el [feh-cha/o-rah]?)

We would be delighted if you could join us - Nos encantaría que te unas a nosotros - (nohs ehn-kahn-tah-ree-ah keh teh oo-nahs a noh-soh-tros)

You're welcome to come - Eres bienvenido/a a venir - (eh-res byen-veh-nee-doh/dah a veh-neer)

I'm sorry, I have another commitment - Lo siento, tengo otro compromiso - (loh see-ehn-toh, ten-go oh-troh kohm-proh-mee-so)

We understand if you can't make it - Entendemos si no puedes venir - (ehn-ten-deh-mohs see noh pweh-des veh-neer)

Let's plan for another time - Planifiquemos para otra ocasión - (plah-nee-fee-keh-mohs pah-rah oh-trah oh-kah-see-on)

We hope you can join us - Esperamos que puedas unirte a nosotros - (eh-speh-rah-mohs keh pweh-das oo-neer-teh a noh-soh-tros)

I accept your invitation - Acepto tu invitación - (ah-sep-toh too een-vee-tah-see-on)

Thank you for thinking of me, but I won't be able to make it - Gracias por pensar en mí, pero no podré asistir - (grah-see-as por pen-sar en mee, peh-roh noh poh-dreh ah-see-teer)

I appreciate the invitation, but I have a prior commitment - Agradezco la invitación, pero tengo un compromiso previo - (ah-grah-des-ko lah een-vee-tah-see-on, peh-roh ten-go oon kohm-proh-mee-so preh-bee-oh)

Discussing Hobbies and Interests

Hobby - Pasatiempo - (pah-sah-tee-ehm-poh)

Interest - Interés - (een-teh-res)

I enjoy... - Disfruto... - (dees-froo-toh)

I like... - Me gusta... - (meh goos-tah)

My hobbies are... - Mis pasatiempos son... - (mees pah-sah-tee-ehm-pohs son)

I'm interested in... - Estoy interesado/a en... - (ehs-toy een-teh-reh-sah-doh/dah en)

What are your hobbies? - ¿Cuáles son tus pasatiempos? - (kwa-les son toos pah-sah-tee-ehm-pohs)

Do you have any special interests? - ¿Tienes algún interés especial? - (tye-nehs ahl-goon een-teh-res es-peh-syal)

I love... - Me encanta... - (meh ehn-kahn-tah)

I'm passionate about... - Me apasiona... - (meh ah-pah-see-oh-nah)

I'm into... - Me interesa... - (meh een-teh-reh-sah)

Playing sports - Jugar deportes - (hoo-gar deh-por-tes)

Painting - Pintar - (peen-tar)

Cooking - Cocinar - (koh-see-nar)

Reading - Leer - (le-er)

Traveling - Viajar - (vee-ah-har)

Photography - Fotografía - (foh-toh-gra-fee-ah)

Dancing - Bailar - (ba-ee-lar)

Playing musical instruments - Tocar instrumentos musicales - (toh-kar een-stroo-men-tos moo-see-kah-les)

Gardening - Jardinería - (har-dee-ne-ree-ah)

Volunteering - Ser voluntario/a - (sehr vol-oon-tah-ree-oh/ah)

Watching TV series - Ver series de televisión - (vehr seh-ree-es deh teh-leh-vee-syon)

Exploring new places - Explorar nuevos lugares - (ehks-plo-rar nwe-vos loo-gah-res)

Learning languages - Aprender idiomas - (ah-prehn-der ee-dyo-mas)

Currency

Currency - Moneda - (moh-neh-dah)

Dollar - Dólar - (doh-lahr)

Euro - Euro - (eh-oo-roh)

Pound - Libra - (lee-brah)

Yen - Yen - (yehn)

Franc - Franco - (frahng-koh)

Rupee - Rupia - (roo-pee-ah)

Yuan - Yuan - (yoo-ahn)

Peso - Peso - (peh-soh)

Rial - Rial - (ree-ahl)

Krona - Corona - (koh-roh-nah)

Baht - Baht - (baht)

Won - Won - (wohn)

Lira - Lira - (lee-rah)

Ruble - Rublo - (roo-bloh)

Swiss Franc - Franco suizo - (frahng-koh swee-soh)

Canadian Dollar - Dólar canadiense - (doh-lahr kah-nah-dyehn-seh)

Australian Dollar - Dólar australiano - (doh-lahr ow-strah-lee-ah-noh)

New Zealand Dollar - Dólar neozelandés - (doh-lahr neh-oh-seh-lahn-dess)

South African Rand - Rand sudafricano - (rahnd soo-dah-free-kah-noh)

Indian Rupee - Rupia india - (roo-pee-ah een-dee-ah)

Brazilian Real - Real brasileño - (reh-ahl brah-see-leh-nyoh)

Mexican Peso - Peso mexicano - (peh-soh meh-hee-kah-noh)

Chinese Yuan - Yuan chino - (yoo-ahn chee-noh)

Japanese Yen - Yen japonés - (yehn hah-poh-ness)

British Pound - Libra esterlina - (lee-brah es-tehr-lee-nah)

Numbers

Zero - Cero - (seh-roh)

One - Uno/Una - (oo-no/oo-nah)

Two - Dos - (dohs)

Three - Tres - (trehs)

Four - Cuatro - (kwah-troh)

Five - Cinco - (seen-koh)

Six - Seis - (sehs)

Seven - Siete - (syeh-teh)

Eight - Ocho - (oh-choh)

Nine - Nueve - (nweh-veh)

Ten - Diez - (dyehs)

Eleven - Once - (ohn-seh)

Twelve - Doce - (doh-seh)

Thirteen - Trece - (treh-seh)

Fourteen - Catorce - (kah-tor-seh)

Fifteen - Quince - (keen-seh)

Sixteen - Dieciséis - (dyeh-see-sehs)

Seventeen - Diecisiete - (dyeh-see-syeh-teh)

Eighteen - Dieciocho - (dyeh-see-oh-choh)

Nineteen - Diecinueve - (dyeh-see-nweh-veh)

Twenty - Veinte - (veh-een-teh)

Thirty - Treinta - (treh-een-tah)

Forty - Cuarenta - (kwa-ren-tah)

Fifty - Cincuenta - (seen-kwen-tah)

Sixty - Sesenta - (seh-sen-tah)

Seventy - Setenta - (seh-ten-tah)

Eighty - Ochenta - (oh-chen-tah)

Ninety - Noventa - (noh-ven-tah)

One hundred - Cien - (syen)

One thousand - Mil - (meel)

One million - Un millón - (oon mee-lyon)

One Billion in Spanish is "Mil Millones" (meel mee-lyo-nes).

Animals

Dog - Perro (peh-roh)

Cat - Gato (gah-toh)

Horse - Caballo (kah-bah-yoh)

Cow - Vaca (bah-kah)

Sheep - Oveja (oh-veh-hah)

Pig - Cerdo (sehr-doh)

Chicken - Pollo (poh-yoh)

Duck - Pato (pah-toh)

Rabbit - Conejo (koh-neh-hoh)

Bird - Pájaro (pah-hah-roh)

Fish - Pez (pehz)

Dolphin - Delfín (dehl-feen)

Lion - León (leh-ohn)

Tiger - Tigre (tee-greh)

Elephant - Elefante (eh-leh-fahn-teh)

Giraffe - Jirafa (hee-rah-fah)

Monkey - Mono (moh-noh)

Bear - Oso (oh-soh)

Wolf - Lobo (loh-boh)

Fox - Zorro (soh-roh)

Snake - Serpiente (ser-pee-en-teh)

Crocodile - Cocodrilo (koh-koh-dree-loh)

Elephant - Elefante (eh-leh-fahn-teh)

Giraffe - Jirafa (hee-rah-fah)

Kangaroo - Canguro (kan-goo-roh)

Penguin - Pingüino (peen-goo-ee-noh)

Octopus - Pulpo (pool-poh)

Butterfly - Mariposa (mah-ree-poh-sah)

Bee - Abeja (ah-beh-hah)

Spider - Araña (ah-rah-nyah)

Bat - Murciélago (moor-see-eh-lah-go)

Squirrel - Ardilla (ar-dee-yah)

Deer - Ciervo (see-ehr-voh)

Shark - Tiburón (tee-boo-rohn)

Parrot - Loro (loh-roh)

Turtle - Tortuga (tor-too-gah)

Jellyfish - Medusa (meh-doo-sah)

Hamster - Hámster (ham-stehr)

Owl - Búho (boo-oh)

Wolf - Lobo (loh-boh)

Deer - Venado (veh-nah-doh)

Bear - Oso (oh-soh)

Monkey - Mono (moh-noh)

Elephant - Elefante (eh-leh-fahn-teh)

Hippopotamus - Hipopótamo (ee-po-poh-tah-moh)

Rhino - Rinoceronte (ree-no-seh-rohn-teh)

Gorilla - Gorila (goh-ree-lah)

Whale - Ballena (bah-yeh-nah)

Crab - Cangrejo (kahn-greh-hoh)

Lobster - Langosta (lahn-gohs-tah)

Flowers

Rose - Rosa (roh-sah)

Lily - Lirio (lee-ree-oh)

Tulip - Tulipán (too-lee-pahn)

Daisy - Margarita (mar-gah-ree-tah)

Orchid - Orquídea (or-kee-deh-ah)

Violet - Violeta (vee-oh-leh-tah)

Carnation - Clavel (klah-vehl)

Daffodil - Narciso (nar-see-soh)

Poppy - Amapola (ah-mah-poh-lah)

Lily of the Valley - Lirio de los Valles (lee-ree-oh deh lohs vah-yes)

Hydrangea - Hortensia (or-ten-see-ah)

Iris - Iris (ee-rees)

Chrysanthemum - Crisantemo (kree-sahn-teh-moh)

Peony - Peonía (peh-oh-nee-ah)

Gerbera - Gerbera (hehr-beh-rah)

Carnation - Clavel (klah-vehl)

Marigold - Caléndula (kah-len-doo-lah)

Azalea - Azalea (ah-sah-leh-ah)

Jasmine - Jazmín (hahz-meen)

Hyacinth - Jacinto (hah-seen-toh)

Daffodil - Narciso (nar-see-soh)

Sunflower - Girasol (hee-rah-sol)

Pronunciation Guide

"a" - pronounced like the "a" in "father"

"e" - pronounced like the "e" in "bed"

"i" - pronounced like the "ee" in "see"

"o" - pronounced like the "o" in "go"

"u" - pronounced like the "oo" in "moon"

"ñ" - pronounced as a separate sound, similar to the "ny" in "canyon"

"ll" - pronounced as a "y" sound, similar to the "y" in "yes"

"r" - pronounced with a single tap of the tongue against the roof of the mouth

"j" - pronounced like the "ch" in "loch" or the "h" in "hat" "qu" - pronounced like the "k" sound followed by a "w" sound

"rr" - pronounced with a rolling or trilling "r" sound

"g" - pronounced like the "g" in "go" before "a", "o", and "u"; like the "h" in "hat" before "e" and "i"

"v" - pronounced like a soft "b" sound

"y" - pronounced like the "y" in "yes"

"x" - pronounced like the "ks" sound in "box"

"b" - pronounced like the English "b" sound

"c" - before "a", "o", and "u" it is pronounced like the English "k" sound;

before "e" and "i", it is pronounced like the "s" sound or the "th" sound in "thin"

"d" - pronounced like the English "d" sound

"f" - pronounced like the English "f" sound

"h" - usually silent in Spanish

"k" - pronounced like the English "k" sound

"m" - pronounced like the English "m" sound

"n" - pronounced like the English "n" sound

"p" - pronounced like the English "p" sound

"s" - pronounced like the English "s" sound

"t" - pronounced like the English "t" sound

Remember, these are just general guidelines, and the pronunciation of certain letters and sounds may vary based on regional accents and dialects. It's always helpful to listen to native speakers or consult audio resources to refine your pronunciation skills.

Printed in Great Britain
by Amazon